MW01121492

BIGGER THAN **JESUS**

BIGGER
THAN **JESUS**

Rick Miller and Daniel Brooks

Bigger Than Jesus
first published 2005 by
Scirocco Drama
An imprint of J. Gordon Shillingford Publishing Inc.
© 2005 Rick Miller and Daniel Brooks

Scirocco Drama Editor: Glenda MacFarlane
Cover design by Terry Gallagher/Doowah Design Inc.
Production photos: glowing bible (page 22), multiple image with apple (page 42),
altar (page 53) , and crown of thorns (page 60) by Cylla von Tiedemann, preacher by
Craig Francis (page 32), crucifixion (page 62) by Beth Kates
Author photos: Rick Miller (Helen Tansey), Daniel Brooks (Cylla von Tiedemann)
Printed and bound in Canada

We acknowledge the financial support of the Manitoba Arts Council, The Canada
Council for the Arts and the Government of Canada through the Book Publishing
Industry Development Program (BPIDP) for our publishing program.

Production inquiries should be addressed to:
WYRD Productions
84 Notre-Dame Ouest, Suite 800
Montreal, QC H2Y 1S6
rick@wyrdproductions.com

Canadian Cataloguing in Publication Data

Miller, Rick, 1970–
  Bigger than Jesus/Rick Miller andDaniel Brooks.

A play.
ISBN 0-920486-86-X

  1. Jesus Christ—Drama. I. Brooks, Daniel, 1958– II. Title.

PS8626.I453B53 2005   C812'.6   C2005-903756-3

J. Gordon Shillingford Publishing
P.O. Box 86, RPO Corydon Avenue, Winnipeg, MB Canada R3M 3S3

To the memory of Christopher Paul Miller

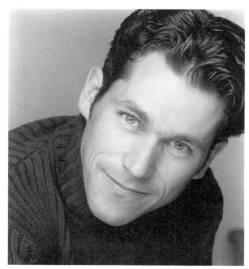

About the Authors

Daniel Brooks is the Artistic Director of The Necessary Angel Theatre Company. He is a prolific and versatile artist whose innovation and risk-taking have made him a leader within the Canadian cultural landscape. His theatrical productions include *Cul-de-Sac, Here Lies Henry, The Noam Chomsky Lectures, Insomnia, The Good Life, Half Life* and *Faust*. The recipient of the inaugural Siminovitch Prize in Theatre (Canada's most prestigious arts award), Brooks' work has toured across the country and the world.

Rick Miller was trained as an architect, actor, and singer, and has performed in three languages on four continents. As the Artistic Director of WYRD Productions, he has created and performed the award-winning shows *Art?, Slightly Bent, Into the Ring* (with playwright Dawson Nichols), and the worldwide hit *MacHomer*. He is one of Canada's most respected multi-disciplinary performers, with credits ranging from classical theatre to the avant-garde, from musicals to live comedy, from voice work to film and television. Miller has also worked extensively with internationally renowned director Robert Lepage on such plays as *La Géométrie des Miracles* and *Zulu Time* (co-created with Peter Gabriel), and on the film *Possible Worlds*.

Production Credits

Bigger Than Jesus was originally developed by the Manitoba Theatre Centre, in association with WYRD Productions, in April 2003. Necessary Angel Theatre Company and WYRD Productions continued its development with workshops throughout the fall of 2003, culminating in workshop productions at Theatre Passe Muraille (Toronto), One Yellow Rabbit's High Performance Rodeo (Calgary) and Catalyst Theatre (Edmonton).

Bigger Than Jesus premiered in Toronto at the Factory Theatre on November 18, 2004, presented by Necessary Angel in association with Factory Theatre with the following creative team:

Created by Rick Miller and Daniel Brooks
Performed by Rick Miller
Directed by Daniel Brooks
Lighting Design by Beth Kates
Sound Design by Ben Chaisson
Video Design by Beth Kates and Ben Chaisson
Production and Stage Managed by Beth Kates
Technical Director: Ben Chaisson
Production Assistant: Vanessa Cassels

Baptism

The stage is a white floor with a large white projection screen hanging upstage. The pre-show music is a medley of songs about Jesus, ending with "Jesus, Wash Away my Troubles," by Sam Cooke. House lights and stage lights go to black. Rick plays an E flat on a pitch pipe, and starts to sing offstage.

I once was lost in sin
But Jesus let me in
And then a little light from heaven
Filled my soul
(Recorded "Filled My Soul.")

Lights up onstage. Rick appears upstage and walks onto the stage barefoot. He is wearing a blue workman's outfit. He plays the pitch pipe note again, and sings:

He bathed my heart in love
And wrote my name above
And then a little talk with Jesus
Made me whole
(Recorded "Made Me Whole.")

Beat. He takes the audience in, and ad libs.

Welcome. What you are about to witness is a Mass. A universal, multi-denominational celebration of Spirit. In this Mass, we will be using the words of the Catholic liturgy, which means there will be lots of references to God. When you hear the word God, you can think whatever you wish to think: a Heavenly Father, the awesome power of Nature, just another three-letter word... It's up to you.

Any Catholics here this evening? Lapsed or unlapsed, it doesn't matter. *(Audience responds.)* You probably know what the liturgy is. For those of you who do not, the Catholic liturgy is the text spoken during the Catholic Mass. What is the Catholic Mass? The Catholic Mass is the celebration of the Eucharist. What is the Eucharist? The Eucharist is the consumption of the body and blood of Jesus Christ to cleanse us of our sins. What is a sin? We'll get to sin later.

The Catholic Mass uses the liturgy to tell a Jesus story. Our Mass this evening will also use the liturgy to tell a Jesus story. In our story, Jesus will teach, he will preach, he will perform miracles on a flight to Jerusalem, he will watch someone die, he will arrive in Jerusalem disheartened, he will get into trouble, he will share a symbolic meal with his followers, he will sing a song that parodies a Broadway musical by Andrew Lloyd-Webber and Tim Rice, he will be arrested, tried, crucified, and resurrected.

Here are a few things you should know about me. I'm 33. I don't believe that Jesus Christ is the Son of God. I don't believe that Christianity is the only way to salvation. I don't know what salvation is, really. I have three older brothers. My mother feels she has failed God because her boys no longer go to Mass. She used to be a sporano. My father, as a young boy, stood with his father and welcomed Hitler into Vienna, as many young boys did with their fathers. My parents lost their fourth child, a three-week old son, before I was born. They decided to have another. That's why I'm here. I will be your Jesus for the evening. Your host... I hope you enjoy the service.

> *He takes a step back, the Mass music begins, the lights shift and Rick begins reciting from the liturgy.*

In the name of the Father, and of the Son,
and of the Holy Spirit. Amen.
The Lord be with you.
(Inviting response from audience.)
And also with you.

My brothers and sisters, to prepare
ourselves to celebrate the sacred mysteries,
let us call to mind our sins.

I confess to almighty God, and to you, my
brothers and sisters, that I have sinned
through my own fault, in my thoughts and
in my words, in what I have done, and in
what I have failed to do; and I ask blessed
Mary, ever virgin, all the angels and saints,
and you, my brothers and sisters, to pray for
me to the Lord our God.

May almighty God have mercy on us,
forgive us our sins, and bring us to
everlasting life. Amen.

Lord, have mercy.
(Inviting response.) Lord have mercy.
Christ, have mercy.
(Inviting response.) Christ, have mercy.
Lord, have mercy.
(Inviting response.) Lord have mercy.

Teacher

*There is a dramatic light and sound change. A
schoolbell rings and Rick kneels down to write on
the white floor, which is being filmed by a video
camera pointing downwards. The image is rear-
projected onto the screen, and flipped so that it is
readable to the audience. He writes an 'I', then an
'S'. then an 'N', spelling 'S-I-N'. He then adds more
letters around the word 'S-I-N', turning it into*

'C-H-R-I-S-T-I-A-N-I-T-Y'. He stands, and begins to teach.

Christianity, ladies and gentlemen. That's our topic for today. It's time to set the record straight, *(He grabs the water bottle, squirting it at the Audience.)* to baptize you all in the Church of rational thought.

He sprays water on the floor, erasing the 'I-T-Y' off 'C-H-R-I-S-T-I-A-N-I-T-Y'.

Made up of CHRISTIANS, followers of one Jesus of Nazareth, named *(Erasing the 'I-A-N' off 'C-H-R-I-S-T-I-A-N'.)* CHRIST by his apostles from the Greek *Christos*, or 'anointed one'. Say, for argument's sake, I'm Jesus. What do we know for CERTAIN about me? First and foremost, I am Jewish. I am a JEW, which may come as a surprise to the 67% of Americans who think that I am a Christian. WRONG! I was born a Jew, I lived a Jew, I died a Jew. There is no evidence that I intended to found a new religion. In fact, Christianity was a Jewish sect until long after my death. What else? I was born into a peasant class, sometime between four and six BC. Yes, Christ was born before Christ. Go figure! What else? Well, from non-Christian sources, the only guy to even mention me in the first hundred years after my death is the Jewish historian Josephus, who, in 90 AD said that I was a wise man who did startling things, had a huge following, came to Jerusalem, was accused of treason, and was crucified by the Romans. EVERYTHING else we think we know about me comes from my followers—a very biased bunch, to say the least—who over the course of 300 years put together a collection of stories and writings called The New Testament. To Christians, The New Testament is a new and improved covenant with God that fulfills the Old covenant with God, the Hebrew Bible, which they call the Old Testament. The New Testament—or TNT as I like to call it—is made up of 27 books, including four books that give accounts of my life and teachings.

He adds 'O-R-Y' to 'C-H-R-I-S-T' to become 'C-H-R-I-S-T-O-R-Y'.

These are called the Gospels, and it is now agreed upon by Christian scholars, archeologists, and other RATIONAL human beings who care to look at facts, that the Gospels were written between forty and a hundred years AFTER my death. Let me be very clear about that. It is highly unlikely that the writers of the four Gospels ever witnessed a single event in my life. The Gospels were pure heresy…hearsay! Sorry.

So we have four different accounts of my life written at four different times by four different people who may have never met me—it's no wonder that these stories constantly CONTRADICT one another. In one book, as I am dying on the cross—my deathbed, so to speak—my final words are, according to Matthew, "My God, My God, why hast thou forsaken me"; according to Luke, "Father, into your hands I commend my spirit"; according to John, "It is finished." Radically different, no? Who's telling the truth? Inquiring minds wanna know! In John's Gospel, Pilate says, "What is truth?" What is 'truth'? 'Truth' is a very difficult word, and it gets abused almost as much as the word 'freedom'. What you have to understand is that the Gospel writers were just that, WRITERS.

He erases 'C' and 'R' from 'C-H-R-I-S-T-O-R-Y'. It becomes 'H-I-S-T-O-R-Y'.

They were not writing HISTORY. When they wrote about the crucifixion, they weren't writing police reports. "The crucifixion…is a fiction!" A fiction of the cross. The Gospels were liturgical proclamations that the living, growing Christian Church needed at that moment to survive. Promotion. Myth-making.

He erases 'H' and 'I', leaving the letters 'S-T-O-R-Y'.

STORY telling. And with any story teller, the thing your hero says as he is dying has tremendous significance on the meaning of the story. What does the writer want you to believe? We in the church of rational thought ask ourselves this question religiously.

Let me try telling a story. The story of a death. We're just outside the city walls of Jerusalem, on the day of my untimely and gruesome crucifixion, which the Romans usually reserve for thieves, rapists, murderers, and enemies of the empire. Here's what it looks like: The landscape is dotted with crosses, not just three crosses, but maybe dozens in close proximity—and on each cross is hung a Jew.

He lies down on stage, facing up at the camera. His full body is projected onscreen.

A stripped, beaten me is thrown to the ground. The Roman Legionnaire feels for the depression at the front of the left wrist, and drives a heavy, square wrought iron nail through the wrist deep into the wood. Wham! Quickly, he moves to the other side to repeat the action. Wham! The transverse bar is then lifted and attached to a tree. The left foot is pressed backward against the right foot. With both feet extended, toes down, a third nail is driven through the arches. Wham! I am now crucified. Ow! Besides the agony of the nails, great waves of cramps sweep over the muscles. The pectoral muscles and the intercostal muscles are unable to act. Air can be drawn into the lungs, but cannot be exhaled. I suffer hours of partial asphyxiation, and searing pain as tissue is torn from my lacerated back from my movement up and down against the rough timbers of the cross. Then another agony begins: a deep crushing pain in the chest as the pericardium, the sac surrounding the heart, slowly fills with serum and begins to compress the heart, which is struggling to pump heavy, thick, sluggish blood to the tissues. Eventually the heart collapses, oxygen no longer reaches the brain, the brain stops functioning, and I die.

He gets up, revealing the word 'S-T-O-R-Y' still written on the floor, and projected onscreen.

That's how we tell a story in the Church of Rational Thought.

Let's go on. I am dead. Normally, when the leader of a movement dies, the movement dies as well. Not so Christianity. My followers are still talking about me, telling stories. Not history. Stories. About what a swell guy I was, how I was full of the Christly wisdom, and how I have been resurrected in their hearts. Figuratively, not literally. As to how a rational human being can believe that a dead body literally comes to life and rises from the ground to the sky, that will be examined in a second year elective, called "The God Part of the Brain: A Darwinian Exploration of Religious Phenomena." Maybe I'll see you there. But for now, let's fast-forward 40 years. The year is 73 A.D. The brutal seven-year rebellion against the Roman Empire has just ended. Jerusalem is decimated. The sacred Temple of the Jews, Solomon's Temple, is reduced to dust, except for one Wall, the Western Wall, the Wailing Wall, still there today. 600,000 Jews have been slaughtered. 600,000 out of maybe 800,000 Jews on the planet. My disciples are scattered or dead. You have to understand the world in which these people lived. These are brutal

times. There is a palpable sense in people's minds
that they are living 'the end of days'. Everywhere
they look is devastation, destruction, inter-
sectarian violence, tribal infighting, ruthless
competition, extremism, TERROR... This is the
context in which the story of me as we have come to
know it is set to paper. This is when the Gospels are
written. And as the Gospels are preached to the
uneducated masses across the Roman Empire,
Christianity slowly transforms from a Jewish sect
to its own religious faith. And one thing that starts
to develop among Christians is Jew hatred. Jew
hatred? I was a Jew, preaching to Jews, using
Jewish concepts! But still, Jew hatred slowly
develops. To show you how, I have to show you
how the four gospels developed.

> *He draws caricatures of Ringo, George, Paul, and*
> *John on the floor.*

The Gospels according to Mark, Matthew, Luke
and John. Ladies and gentlemen, "The Beatles."
The Evangelist Mark—the Beatle Ringo: the oldest,
the shortest, builds a solid rhythm for the others,
nothing flashy. Matthew—George: more spiritual,
occasionally adds a composition of his own to the
mix. Luke—Sir Paul: the chatty one, the friendly
one. Everyone likes Luke, everyone likes Paul.
They have prolific solo careers. Luke writes "Acts
of the Apostles," Paul writes "Band on the Run."
John—John: the poet, more controversial than the
rest. Gets himself and others into trouble. These
three *(Circles Paul, George and Ringo.)* are similar
enough in style, tone, and story elements to be
grouped together. Scholars call them the Synoptic
Gospels *(Writes 'synoptics'.)*. John's Gospel is a
completely different animal. There are two things
that are developed and exaggerated in John that
have had disastrous consequences for the Jews.
One is the repeated insistence that I am literally the

Son of God, and that the only way to God is through me, his Son. If you do not believe that I am the Son of God, you reject the salvation offered by God via his Son, you reject God, and you are therefore damned. The second thing that develops in John is that the Jews become Christ killers. Me killers. In the earlier Gospels, the Jews are mentioned, but not in such blatantly antagonistic terms. For example, in Mark, it's "the crowd" that sets itself against me. Then, in Matthew, it evolves into "the people", with Pilate the Roman washing his hands clean of guilt. John's Gospel seals the deal by actually blaming "the Jews" directly for my death:

Pilate said to the Jews, "Here is your King!"
The Jews cried out, "Kill him! Kill him! Crucify him!" *(John 19:15)*

Remember that John's Gospel was written last, meaning that this is what developed over time. Why? Because as more and more Romans are converted to Christianity, blaming the Jews for my crucifixion is becoming more and more convenient. Blaming the Romans doesn't make much sense anymore, especially if you want to stay off of trees. So, the Jewish origins of Christianity become more and more obscure with each Gospel. By the time John's is done, Rome and the Christians share a common enemy: the Jews.

And if we had more time, I would take great pleasure in tracing a line of anti-Semitic cause and effect from the Crucifixion all the way to the Holocaust. How could a crucifed Jew trigger centuries of anti-semitism? That's a third year elective. For now, may I just say that in the 1960s, after almost 2000 years of blaming the Jews for killing me, the Catholic Church at Vatican II finally chose to shift the blame back to the Romans—who invented crucifixion in the first place—but the damage had been done, folks. John's version was the one that stuck in people's heads, hearts and mouths for almost two millennia.

So. Let's say 2000 years have passed. Let's say I have seen everything. Let's say I have cameras, computers, remote controls. I've been watching from my control tower since my death. I speak all languages, and have access to all the information out there about me. What do I see? I see crucifixes on walls in homes in countries all over the world. I see a very old man in Rome still claiming to speak infallibly in my name. I see a Christian fundamentalist in charge of the world's only dominant empire, frighteningly certain in his belief that we are living in 'the end of days'. What else do I see? I see millions of works of art, thousands of books, hundreds of hit singles, and two Broadway musicals! Gosh-gee! How did I, a country rabbi, come to be worshipped 2000 years after my death?

He turns the camera off with a remote control.

For a story to evolve like this, it has to be seductive in the first place. Seduction is an integral part of storytelling. Macbeth is a far more seductive character as a tragic villain than as a good king who ruled for 17 years of peace and prosperity, which he did. Similarly, I am a far more seductive as the crucified Son of God offering universal salvation than as yet another victim of imperial power. Fine. But as long as we have a significant portion of the civilized world that believes that these STORIES are the true, historical, literal word of God, and— even worse—the only way to God, I think we have a serious problem. The world would be a much safer place if Christians read their Bible as beautiful and inspiring literature.

Choral music. He puts the marker and spray bottle

down. He slowly walks stage right. A Bible is handed to him. He walks back centre with it. He holds the Bible above his head, facing upstage. The cross on the Bible glows. He turns, lowers the Bible, and opens it.

A reading from the Holy Gospel according to Matthew. Glory to you, Lord.

"And seeing the multitudes, he went up into the mountain: and when he had sat down, his disciples came unto him. And he lifted up his eyes on his disciples and he opened his mouth, and taught them, and said, Blessed are the poor in spirit: for theirs is the kingdom of heaven.
Blessed are they that mourn: for they shall be comforted.
Blessed are the meek: for they shall inherit the earth.
Blessed are they who hunger and thirst after righteousness: for they shall be filled.
Blessed are the merciful: for they shall obtain mercy.
Blessed are the pure in heart: for they shall see God.
Blessed are the peacemakers: for they shall be called sons of God.
Blessed are they that have been persecuted for righteousness' sake: for theirs is the kingdom of heaven.
Rejoice ye in that day, and be exceeding glad: and leap for joy: for behold, your reward is great in heaven."

This is the Gospel of the Lord. Thanks be to God.

Preacher

Blackout. He places the Bible on the floor. A camera, set in a triangular frame, descends from above. It points down at the glowing crucifix on the Bible. We see the glowing crucifix projected onscreen. He begins to preach.

When I was growing up, the eye of God was everywhere. We had crucifixes all over the house. In my room, there was one crucifix. A glow-in-the-dark crucifix. And it glowed so bright, I couldn't sleep at night. So I took it down, and put up a mirror.

Rick tilts the camera from the Bible to his eyes.

Momma was real mad. She called me the 'Fallen Son', and my brothers, they all laughed at me, and called me the 'ego-tist'. But they didn't understand that I wasn't lookin'AT someone, I was lookin' FOR someone. Now if y'all are thinking this is sermon time, y'all are right. And if y'all are thinkin' sermon time means nap time, y'all are wrong.

He tilts the camera to his mouth.

Cuz in my Church, Sermon time is WAKE-UP time!

Rousing music begins. Rick gets everyone clapping, and eventually stops. He goes behind the camera, turns out the light, and zooms in on various audience members.

I look at the people sitting before me and what do I see? I see bright, shiny faces thinking "I didn't know this was gonna be one of them inter-active plays."

He steps away from the camera, and moves towards the audience. The camera is behind him. We see his back projected onscreen as he moves about energetically.

I look beyond the blinking eyes and po-lite stares, and I see a people so sleepy they don't even know they're asleep. And y'all are saying: "Hey! I'm not asleep! Look, my eyes are open!" But I'm not talking about your eyes here *(Pointing to his eyes.)*, nonono. I'm talking about your eye *here (Pointing to his heart.).* Your heart. Your Spirit. Your Capital 'I' eye. The one that makes you, YOU. The one that makes I, I! Your Jesus is asleep! And some of thinkin' "Oh, man, he's gonna start talking about that Jesus crap." Well, you can call it what you want: Jesus, Buddha, Allah, Yahweh, Zeus…Bob. Doesn't matter to me. What matters to me is that it's sleepy. Your Jesus is asleep. And my Jesus says, "Blessed are the sleepy, for theirs is the Kingdom of Heaven." Did Jesus say that? My Jesus says whatever the hell he wants! And My Jesus tells me that the Kingdom of Heaven isn't some magical Jerusalem that the "chosen few" will go live in, after Super-Jesus flies down one last time to kick the shit out of Satan. My Jesus says that's crap! The Kingdom of Heaven is not promised, it's already here, in your heart! So rejoice, be glad, and leap for joy! But there's one problem: in order to reach your Kingdom of Heaven, you sleepy people need to wake your Jesus up. I can't wake him up for you, but I can wake YOU up, and then YOU can wake your Jesus up yourselves. So let me roll up my sleeves, cuz I know that I have some work to do. And so do you. Y'all better clear that crap outta your throats now, and warm up that sleepy voice, cuz ya'll got four words to say: "Hey Jesus! Wake up!" At the count of three: One, two, three… *(The audience meekly says, "Hey Jesus, wake up.")* Oh, come on. Jesus just pressed the snooze button. C'mon, use your balls! You ladies, use your vaginas! One, two, three. *(The audience yells, "Hey*

Jesus! Wake up!") One more time! (*The audience yells, "Hey Jesus! Wake up!"*) Halleluia! Jesus is opening his eyes, wiping the crud out of the corners, scratching his ass. Aaaaah! Welcome to the Church of YOU!! Congratulations! Your Jesus is awake!… Now what?

You gotta keep him awake. And how? By doing lots of livin'! Keep movin', don't get stuck in one place! It's only natural to keep things movin'! Look around you. Everythin's movin'. I'm movin' all over the place. (*Turns to camera, and moves furiously back and forth.*) Your eyeballs movin', tryin' to keep up with me. We got planes, trains, automobiles buzzin' around. The continents are movin', the earth is spinnin' on its axis, and rotatin' round the Sun, and the Solar System's spinnin' around the Milky Way, which is still shootin' off from some big gang orgy billions of years ago! Wow! And look inside you. Everythin's movin' too. Your Jesus is pumpin', your blood is flowin', your hormones and your enzymes all workin' in there. Last night's dinner will be comin' out soon enough. All them steak and potatoes and green beans, or tofu. (*Grunts with delight.*) It's movin' all right. Even our stories are movin', they be constantly changin', growin', evolvin' as we speak. Nothing is fixed. Cuz' when somethin' gets fixed, it gets sleepy. Jesus looked at those old, sleepy stories of his time, those laws, and he woke them up! He set them FREE. Cuz you gotta be free. You don't want no strings attached. My limbs are free, my tongue is free, my grammar is free. The Church of ME is free! In MY world, it's not called religion, it's called DANCIN'! Gimme some music!

Funky music. He dances.

Wooooo! (*He continues dancing with more spirit.*) WOOHOO! C'mon, brothers and sisters, lemme see your hands in the air.

He gets everyone to raise their arms and shake them to the music… He gets them to stop.

…Sheep!

(He smells his own sweat.) Aaaaah! The smell of livin'! *(He sprays his sweat at the audience.)* I baptize you in the Church of ME! Haha! Now let me tell you a bit about the Church of Me. The Church of Me ain't got nothin' to do with *(Into camera, his face big onscreen.)* Christianity *(Then away from camera.).* The Church of Me doesn't deny nature, it embraces it. What's natural is that shit happens. This is a messed up world, full of messed up people, like me, like you, like Jesus, who saw that suffering was part of the natural order, something we gotta learn to live with, not the result of "Original Sin." Original Sin. What the hell is that? You're telling me that 6000 years ago, some guy bit into an apple that some naked chick gave him, and from that point on all of humanity was cursed with mortality, and the beautiful baby coming out of my wife's loins is a sinner, by some genetic defect called original sin? What?! And that if that baby dies before some priest splashes water on him, he's stuck in some place called 'limbo' for eternity? Fuck off! That's just abstract shit that some old man invented to keep me scared. Cuz if I'm scared, he can do whatever the hell he wants with me. He's got me under his control. He's got the power of God in his hands. And if he also happens to have my ass in his hands, that's probably my fault for having such a sweet ass! Get your fuckin' hands off me, asshole! I'm not buying into that 'Doctrine of Sin' shit. I don't even understand it. What is it? I'm allowed to sin, …or no, I'm condemned to sin because of Original Sin, and that when I sin I should feel guilty for being tempted by the Devil, and then I gotta feel contrition or something, and then I gotta go repent and confess my sins, no, but

wait...there's venial sin and mortal sin, and when I die I have to wait in purgatory for the last judgement to see if I will be granted God's mercy to be saved...or go be eternally damned in the fires of hell with all the faggots and the feminists and the A-rabs... Aw, shut up! That shit has nothing to do with Jesus. At least not my Jesus. My Jesus don't believe in sin. Now this does not mean I go around rapin' and pillagin'... I do not live in a moral vacuum! My morality is my guiding light, that's my Jesus, it's my sense of what is right and what is wrong, what will adversely affect me/others/the planet and what will not. I don't believe in an abstract concept, I believe in me, all 5'10" of sweatin', stupid me and my natural instincts. And my natural instincts tell me to take the word SIN, and throw away the S, throw away the N. What you got left? I! And I take that I and I ride it for all its worth. *(He pretends to ride a long straight 'I', stroking it shamelessly.)* That's where I'm at. The I at the centre. Where I got perspective. I can see both sides of every story. I'm not stuck on one side, saying "I'm right...you're left...I'm good, you're evil...I'm Christian, you're Muslim...I'm black, you're white." NO, you wanna be at the Centre, at the union of dualities, like that Zen symbol with the black and the white, and the little nipples on either side. The place to be is at the centre, where it's warm and wet, and where the creative juices are flowin', and where we got good and evil, God and Devil scrappin' with each other all the time, givin' us CHOICES every second of our lives. I got lots of choices right now. I could kick this thing right here, but that would hurt my foot. I'm not gonna do that. That's a choice I just made. I could take a dump in the lobby, but y'all gonna step in that later, and that's kinda gross. I'm not gonna do that. That's a choice I just made. I could go and kiss that guy over there on the lips, but... Aw, what the hell!

He goes to kiss a man in the audience. On the lips.
He returns to the stage.

See, your choices can have an EFFECT on the world. That guy either wants to slap me, or he's kind of horny, I dunno. But those are EASY choices. Everybody has harder choices too. Like "What are you gonna do with your life?" or "Who are you gonna live your life with?" or "Are you gonna bring a child into this messed up, crazy-ass world?" Those are the hard choices. And here's one more. Everybody knows somebody who's all bunged up with grief and anger cuz they lived a harder life than you, and they let you know every chance they get: "I lived a harder life than you!" And they all crusty and stiff all the time, with their shoulders up to their earlobes, cursing everything. And they get into their car, *(Taking the wheel.)* but it's not a car, it's a Ford Toro-Exploro-Bronco-Humvee big-ass shit, and it's like 20 yards long and 16 yards wide, and they drive to work going "I feel safe in my car! Don't look at me like that! You don't know what kinda life I lived!" And they get to the parking lot, down to P1 *(He spins.)* P2 *(He spins.)* P3 *(He spins.)* P4, and they going "I hate this place! *(Getting out of a tight parking space.)* Don't touch my car!" And they get into the elevator, *(Squeezing in.)* but there are other people around. "I hate people! They don't know what kinda life I lived." And then they get into a little cubicle, not makin' eye contact with nobody, and they open up their little laptop and they play solitaire… Everybody knows somebody like that! And the hard choice is this: "Do you not talk to that person, or do you talk to that person?" If you do, then one of two things could happen. They either tell you to "fuck off," or the floodgates gonna open, and you're gonna have a "high-maintenance friend," right? But your choice can have a huge effect on that person. Our choices are a gift, because our choices can have an effect. Yeah. See, that person is suffering. We know that. It's what we all got in common. We all suffer, every last one of us, and then we die. End of story. And you can think whatever the hell you want about an afterlife for your soul, but the hard fact of the matter is that your hot, sweaty body will get cold and start to rot, and if you haven't had any effect on anybody before you die, you certainly won't have an effect on anybody AFTER you die. You are RESPONSIBLE for the effect you have in this life. You have a RESPONSIBILITY. So you have to EDUCATE your responsibility. And how do you educate your responsibility? By educating your IMAGINATION! By reading stories, going to the theatre, going to the art gallery, to a Church or a Synagogue or a Temple, wherever your mind is free to roam. By playing music, by playing in the sand, by playing with your CHILDREN, who aren't stupid and sleepy yet. Then you start to imagine a kind of CONNECTION, a relationship with everybody and everything. Between all those dualities, between me and this camera, between me and you. Your relationship to whoever is next to you, to your mother back home, to your kids, your lover, your boss. That's why people go to the theatre, to Church even, is to establish some form of relationship, some connection, some COMMUNION. A COMMON…UNION with other suffering souls, whose 'I's are as sleepy as yours. But then somebody opens your 'I' up, and tells you you gotta LIVE your life, not let somebody else tell you how to live it. You gotta live your life, and you gotta live it with PASSION. That's what this is all about Brothers and sisters, … PASSION. PASSION. PASS-I-ON. PASS-I-ON. My Jesus' passion story, is a story of PASS-I-ON. He took his 'I' and he passed it on so far that it reached me. Now that's havin' an EFFECT! "I Am", said Jesus. Two most important words of the Bible. I AM, I AM! I don't need hope/faith in the beyond,

in the Kingdom come! I AM! And I AM standing
right here, right now, speaking these words to you.

I am the Word
I am the Word made flesh
I give myself to you through passion and spirit and
sweat
I give myself to you who are crucifed every day of
your life by your church, by your country, by your
job, by your family, by yourselves
If you are hungry, take me into you
Take my body into you
And swallow me whole, digest me, consume me
Feel me burning inside you
You are now of me
You are good and evil, God and Devil
You are Jesus
You are the one baptised anew
You are the one teaching, preaching, makin'
miracles
You are the one offerin' yourself
You have died and been resurrected
Your I has come to life, you who have slept so long
And now you will pass your I on
PASS YOUR I ON
PASS YOUR I ON
HALLELUIA!
HALLELUIA!
HALLELUIA!

> *The video image of Rick's arms outspread in praise*
> *is frozen onscreen. The living Rick slowly takes his*
> *arms down, and continues with the liturgy.*

I believe in God, *(Many recorded voices speak*
the liturgy with him.) the Father almighty,
creator of heaven and earth.

> *He buttons his shirt as the image onscreen behind*
> *him fades. The voiceover continues with him.*

I believe in Jesus Christ, his only Son, our Lord. He was conceived by the power of the Holy Spirit and born of the Virgin Mary. He suffered under Pontius Pilate, was crucified, died and was buried. He descended to the dead. On the third day he rose again, He ascended into heaven, and is seated at the right hand of the Father. He will come again to judge the living and the dead.

He hesitates, and then stops speaking. The voiceover continues without him.

I believe in the Holy Spirit, the holy Catholic Church, the communion of saints, the forgiveness of sins, the resurrection of the body, and the life everlasting. Amen. *(Rick says.)* Amen.

He turns to the flying camera upstage.

Blessed are you, Lord, God of all creation.

He approaches the camera and manipulates it.

Through your goodness we have this to offer, which earth has given and human hands have made. I will become for us the bread of life. Blessed be God forever.

He sends the camera up into the lights.

Blessed are you, Lord, God of all creation. Through your goodness we have this to offer, fruit of the vine and work of human hands. It will become our spiritual drink. Blessed be God for ever.

May the Lord accept the sacrifice at your hands for the praise and glory of his name, for our good, and the good of all his Church.

Miracles

Rick flips the Bible over, opens it up, and it transforms into a laptop. He speaks into a camera hidden inside.

We pray to the Lord.
(Computer voice.) Lord, hear our prayer.

We hear a plane taking off as Rick slides a crucifix over the hidden camera. The flying crucifix is projected onscreen. He leaves the laptop on the floor, and closes the lid.

Good evening, ladies and gentlemen, and welcome aboard Air Jesus Flight 1234, a one-way non-stop flight experience from Toronto to Jerusalem, the eternal city. We will be flying through some difficult airspace, and so we ask you to please keep your suspension of disbelief securely fastened, and your emotional baggage safely stowed underneath your seats or in the overhead compartments. My name is Jesus, but think of my right now as your Cosmic Christ, helping you navigate through some of life's mysteries. My primary goal is to answer your prayers and bring you comfort on your journey to Jerusalem. But if we have time, we can chat about some of the larger questions that hover around us. Heck, maybe I'll even perform a few miracles! Oh! One more thing before we get cracking: why an airplane? Well, airplanes are very interesting, sociologically speaking. People pray more in airplanes. *(Goes to pick up the laptop.)* And thanks to the miracle of modern technology, we have satellite access to every single prayer on every single Air Jesus flight to Jerusalem. Ladies and gentlemen, may I introduce the Prayer-Cam.

He opens the laptop lid. A choir sings a heavenly chord.

I love this thing. Lemme demonstrate how it works. Let's go in for a prayer.

He looks down at the camera, or "Prayer-Cam", hidden in the laptop. A bell dings.

Ah! Flight 679 from Las Vegas just took off. Always lots of fresh prayers on that one. Let's go to seat 33B, male, 42, named George. He's paralyzed.

Rick looks into the Prayer-Cam. His face is projected onscreen.

JESUS: Hi, George.

GEORGE: Jesus fucking Chri–

JESUS: No need for that George. I'm here. What can I do for you?

GEORGE   I hate turbulence!

JESUS: Don't we all, George… Now look. Settle down and tell me what the problem is.

GEORGE: *(Whines.)*

JESUS: Spit it out, George. I know about the affair.

GEORGE: What have I done?

JESUS: George, it's not about what you've done, it's about what you're gonna do. What are you gonna do?

GEORGE: I…

JESUS: I'll tell you what you're gonna do. When this plane lands, you're gonna drive home, take your kids to your mother-in-law's, come back, sit your wife in her favourite chair, pour her her favourite drink, and tell her everything.

GEORGE: Everything?

JESUS: Yes, everything, George. How long it's been. How many times. Who else knows. And it's going to be hard, especially on her. And she'll probably want to hit you, or leave you... I can't tell. But it's what you have to do. Understand? *(Pause.)* I'll put in a good word for you. OK?

GEORGE: *(Shakes his head.)* OK.

We pray to the Lord.
(Computer voice.) Lord, hear our prayer.

Rick closes the lid of the laptop. Images of a moving sky and clouds appear onscreen. He walks downstage.

How many adulterers on this flight? *(Pause.)* I know, I know, I'm putting you on the spot. Well, for those of you who are adulterers or who have been in the past, "Be of good cheer; your sins are forgiven you." You're forgiven. There. Forgiveness is easy. And why is it easy? Well, to answer that question we'll have to go back 13.7 billion years. 13.7 billion years ago, everything in the Universe is compressed into a tiny little package of matter. In that package of matter are the laws of the Universe, the laws of the God, the laws of physics, whatever you wanna call 'em. And then, in a moment, faster than George can say, "Come up to my room and I'll show you how this thing works," BOOM, the Big Bang. Cosmic dust shoots off in all directions. Then gravity immediately starts condensing the dust into galaxies. In one of the spiral arms of one of the galaxies, a relatively large dust ball ignites at the core, becoming a star, our beloved Sun. Smaller dust balls in the neighborhood condense into comets, asteroids, and planets. One of these planets, the third from the sun, through a series of events—call them miracles if you like—eventually develops Life. Single-celled organisms evolve into multi-celled organisms, which evolve into fish, reptiles, chimps, homo this homo that, and finally homo sapiens, who learns to control fire, and invents tools, temples, weapons, the wheel, the printing press, and—miracle of miracles—the airplane, and in one such airplane, only moments ago, a man named George just sent a prayer to Jesus because of a little dalliance with his boss. He will land, he will confess to his wife, they will work things out as best they can, and then George will die, his wife will die, their children will die, and I hate to break it to you, but all of humanity will die as well. I can't tell you how, exactly, but there will be wailing and gnashing of teeth...and the Universe will continue to dance its inexplicable little dance without us. And the sooner you can get your head around that, the easier it is to forgive.

He does a little dance.

I should get back to work. I've got prayers to answer.

He opens the laptop lid. A bell rings.

Nice, clear prayer from Flight 1313 from Paris, Oh la la, seat 15C, young girl named Julie. *(Rick walks behind screen.)* She seems to be blind.

Rick looks into the Prayer-Cam. We see the shadow of his body and the image of his face projected onscreen.

JESUS: Oui, Julie.

JULIE: Je t'aime, Jesus.

JESUS: Je t'aime aussi, Julie. C'est quoi le probleme?

JULIE: Je t'AIME. Je t'aime je t'aime je t'aime enormement.

JESUS: Julie, qu'est-ce qu'il y a?

JULIE: Je t'aime.

JESUS: Et tu aimes quelqu'un d'autre, n'est-ce pas?.

JULIE: Oui.

JESUS: Tu l'aimes beaucoup.

JULIE: Oui.

JESUS: Et ne veux pas me trahir.

JULIE: Oui.

JESUS: Julie, je serai toujours la avec toi, en Esprit. Quel est son nom?

JULIE: *(Beat.)* Marie-Therese.

JESUS: Ah! Julie, ecoute-moi bien. Un jour, quand tu te sens completement bien avec Marie-Therese, laisse-toi aller. L'amour, c'est un miracle. Il n'y a pas plus simple que cela. Ouvre tes yeux, Julie, et laisse-toi aller.

JULIE: Je t'aime.

We pray to the Lord.
(Computer voice.) Lord, hear our prayer.

He closes the laptop lid and emerges from behind screen. Images of sky and cloud appear onscreen, but more mysterious this time.

Coffee, tea, or miracles? Ah... Love is a miracle. Life is a miracle. In the beginning there was nothing, and before you know it...there's a Pope! With a laptop! *(Typing.)* "Congratulations! You've become a Saint."

You wanna know how people become Saints? It's very interesting. You have to die a martyr, or you have to perform two Vatican-sanctioned miracles. It used to be three, but Pope John Paul II lowered the bar to only two, because Saints are good for business. *(Beat.)* Did you know that in his 25 years on the job, he beatified and sanctified almost 1000 lucky Catholics? That's about one a week.

Anyway, it seems the new Pope has placed John Paul II on the fast-track to Sainthood, just as his predecessor did with another media superstar, Mother Teresa. And so the usual five-year waiting period will be waived, the petitioners for his Sainthood will present evidence of two miracles, the Vatican will send the Miracle Police, who will get together over a round of Bloody Marys, presumably, to determine whether the miracles are *scientifically inexplicable*. If they are deemed so, then Catholics can begin praying to Saint John Paul, assuming his petitioners have raised the half a million bucks or so that the Vatican charges for the service.

I don't mean to pick on Popes. It must be hard when some people believe that God speaks through you. But there are others who believe that God speaks through the President of the United States. There are others who believe that God speaks through Michael Moore, a fat Messiah in a ballcap. And there may even be some who believe that God speaks through me, Jesus, talking about miracles on a metaphoric flight to Jerusalem.

He does a little dance again.

Is it Prayer-Cam time?

Looks down at the laptop. A bell rings.

OK…Flight— Well, whaddya know! It's this flight right here. Man, age 33, name is Rick. He's possessed.

Rick looks into the Prayer-Cam. His face is projected onscreen.

JESUS: Rick, what can I do ya for? Haven't heard from you in a while.

RICK: I've been busy. Listen, there's this kind of Mass I'm doing. It's about halfway through—

Big sound and light disturbance.

FEEDBACK FEEDBACK FEEDBACK.

He closes the laptop lid. He places the laptop down and looks into another camera placed on the floor downstage. It creates a multiple image of Rick onscreen, like a double mirror effect. Rick speaks into the camera.

That was unexpected. Or was it? Maybe it's part of the script. Part of the Master Plan. Maybe everything that has happened, is happening and will happen, from Adam swallowing the Apple to Keanu swallowing the red pill, everything has been pre-determined, and we are all just actors in a divine comedy. The question then becomes 'who wrote the script?', and 'where can I get a copy?' It's on sale in the lobby for 10 bucks.

He gets up from kneeling, and picks up an apple from in front of the camera.

Or maybe there is no script. Maybe everything that happens is not pre-determined.

He slowly backs toward the screen.

Maybe we're all free to act as we will. That means that every choice we make changes the course of history. That biting into an apple in Toronto can cause a plane to crash into Jerusalem. Cause *(Video effect.)* and effect *(Video effect.)* Cause *(Video effect.)* and effect *(Video effect.)* So is there a script or not? Can't tell ya. But what I can tell ya is this: *(Tossing apple into the air.)* What goes up, must come down.

Takes a bite of the apple. Turbulence.

Well, speak of the Devil. Seems one of our flights is

going down. I'd better go take care of that one.

He goes to the laptop and picks it up. The multiple-image effect stops. Sky and clouds appear onscreen again, stranger than ever.

I know you have many choices for prayer travel, and so on behalf of Air Jesus, I would like to thank you for your continued faith. And if Jerusalem is your final destination, have yourselves a great day. So let's go to a prayer on that ill-fated flight.

He looks down a tthe laptop. A bell rings.

A woman, age 68, she's staring out the window. *(To audience.)* Let's go down with Grace.

Rick looks into the Prayer-Cam. His face is projected onscreen.

JESUS: Hi, Grace.

GRACE: Hello.

JESUS: Mind if I sit with you?

GRACE: Not at all. *(Pause.)*

JESUS: You know this plane's going to crash.

Grace nods.

Is there anything I can do for you?

GRACE: Take care of my children.

JESUS: Rest in peace, Grace.

Turbulence builds.

GRACE: Amen.

There is a brief moment of silence, and then an enormous crash. Rick closes the laptop and a thin stream of sand falls from the ceiling. Images flash on the screen—a quick succession of photos of faces and families and weddings and wars—as the sand continues to fall and the sound of the crash settles. The sand collects on the stage. Rick puts down the laptop, kneels upstage of the sand and puts his hand in the stream that still falls from above. The images have ceased flashing, replaced by static. The camera begins to descend. The static fades and we see the stream of sand projected onscreen. The camera follows the stream of sand as it descends to the floor.

"And I saw a new heaven and a new earth; for the first heaven and the first earth passed away… And I saw the holy city, new Jerusalem, coming down out of heaven from God…and there shall no longer be any death; there shall no longer be any mourning, or crying, or pain; the first things have passed away." *(Revelation 21:1-4)*

The camera continues its slow descent. We see the sand falling in multiple-image effect. The camera finally settles on the floor. Rick puts his hand in the sand pile, then manipulates the camera, preparing for Jerusalem. We hear a mixture of both Muslim and Jewish chanting as Rick continues with the liturgy.

Holy, holy, holy Lord, God of power and might, heaven and earth are full of your glory. Hosanna in the highest. Blessed is he who comes in the name of the Lord. Hosanna in the highest.

Jerusalem/Last Supper

We see Rick's hands and knees, and a large pile of sand projected onscreen.

Jesus came to Jerusalem.

He reaches into the laptop box and pulls out a Jesus action figure. He walks it into frame.

He came to be arrested, tried, and crucified by the Roman Empire. He wasn't committing suicide; he was sacrificing himself as a symbol of love, to give hope to all who are oppressed. Like Obi-Wan Kenobi in *Star Wars*, which was one of Jesus' favourite movies. His Mom brought him to it when he was seven years old, and he loved it so much, he chose his disciples from among the characters in the movie. The Father,

Pulls out a Darth Vader action figure.

The Son,

He pulls out a Luke Skywalker action figure.

And the Holy Ben Kenobi.

He pulls out an Obi-Wan Kenobi action figure. He places them all in the sand.

So once in Jerusalem, being devout Jews, he and his disciples go straight to the Temple,

He places a large card with an image of the Western Wall behind the action figures.

which has turned into a bustling marketplace where everything is for sale: Jesus action figures, Jesus coffee mugs, boxer shorts that say "What Would Jesus Do?" And what Jesus does is he gets very angry, flips the tables, and cries out "...My temple should be a house of prayer, but you have made it into a den of thieves! Get out! Get out!" The soldiers arrive.

Rick pulls out a toy soldier.

His disciples are poised to defend him, but Jesus stops them. "My time has not yet come," he says, with that air of gravity and mystery that he has perfected over the years. He knows that he will be handed over to the authorities, who will put him to death. But not yet.

He walks the soldier off.

First, there is a Passover meal to be celebrated.

He pulls out a small wooden ruler and lays it out in the sand as a table. Each subsequent action figure is placed behind the ruler, echoing 'The Last Supper'.

So he invites all his friends to sit at the Pesach table. The Reverend,

He pulls out a Martin Luther King Jr. action figure.

The pacifist,

He pulls out a Gandhi action figure.

The prostitute,

He pulls out an action figure of Dorothy from The Wizard of Oz.

Her pimp,

He pulls out and action figure of the Tinman from The Wizard of Oz.

And of course Judas.

He pulls out a Homer Simpson 'Pez' dispenser.

Then a special guest walks in.

He pulls out a John Lennon action figure.

Jesus and John Lennon had had a falling out many years ago, and so there is much tension and complete silence. Except for Darth Vader's breathing, which he can't help. And then...

John approaches Jesus.

JOHN: I am you and you are me, as you are he and we are all together.

JESUS: Googoogachoo?

JOHN: Googoogachoo.

          They embrace.

Everyone is overjoyed.

          Jesus pats John on the bum.

Jesus sends John to the back, because he's just a little bit bigger than everyone else, and he calls for some entertainment. The Reverend and the Mahatma have a debating contest about the nature of power in a post-colonial world.

          They do so.

Then, the prostitute and her pimp do that amazing trick with the oil can.

          They do so.

Then, his disciples perform a key scene from one of their movies:

          They do so.

DARTH: Luke, Obi-Wan never told you what happened to your father.

LUKE: He told me you killed him.

DARTH: No. I am your father.

Everyone is giddy with joy, and Jesus calls them back to the table, and says: "But seriously. One of you here will betray me."

Pause. Homer Simpson 'Pez' Dispenser looks to the left, to the right, then sneaks off.

Aware that he has dampened the mood somewhat, Jesus hops over the table, and walks out into the garden of Gethsemane to clear his head. And suddenly, he has a vision.

A second Jesus action figure confronts Jesus.

2nd JESUS: Everything that has transpired has done so according to my design, young Nazarene. There is no escape from your destiny. Now... you...must...die.

The second Jesus flies off with a 'whoosh'.

More confused than ever, Jesus heads back inside.

Jesus hops over the table.

Terrible images begin to crowd his head: soldiers hammering nails, shattering bone. Vultures feasting on human flesh. He looks at the bread on the table and sees his battered body. He looks at the wine and sees blood pouring from his wounds. He hops up onto the table—very carefully, because he's had quite a bit to drink—looks directly into the camera, and calls for music.

Arrest

> *The Jesus action figure sings a parody of 'Gethsemane' from "Jesus Christ Superstar."*

I know you're here.
With me, within me.
A Father's hand controls my fate.

> *A snake slides into frame.*

I hear the hiss, I smell the poison,
I don't think I can bear the weight.

> *The snake slithers off, Jesus hops down from the table.*

Take this cup away from me,
I tremble from the taste.

> *Jesus moves forward.*

Tell me all that I've accomplished won't be laid to waste.

> *Jesus moves forward.*

Thirty years and three have passed,
Have they all been flawed?

> *Jesus moves forward, and keeps going until he disappears.*

I feel so small and human,

> *He reappears in extreme close-up.*

Who am I to question God?

> *He turns away, dramatically, and then turns back.*

Is this your will?

> *He returns to the table. A soldier enters, searching.*

The soldiers come.

They're looking for me.

The soldier disappears.

And here I stand scared stiff with fear.

Jesus hops forward on every beat.

They will hate me, hit me, hurt me, curse me, crush me, kill me.

He turns away from the camera.

My crucifixion's drawing near.

Musical bridge.

I see the future,

> *A card appears behind him with an image of Jesus action figures on display.*

And it looks like hell.

New card: Jesus selling Coca-Cola.

My image on billboards.

New card: "Jesus Saves."

And movies by Mel.

> *New card: Mel Gibson speaking to actor playing Jesus on film set.*

This beast will become so much bigger than me.

Jesus pushes last card aside.

What's to be learnt here?
What's in it for me?

Does a big windmill guitar strum.

Tell me who I am, my God,

He sways side to side.

And what am I to do?
Why have I to bear this cross?

He shakes his head.

Where the hell are you?

He runs to the left.

I'm the one they'll torture,

He runs to the right.

It's my face drenched in blood,

He runs off. Immediately, the second Jesus appears.

It's my cross on my shoulders
as I drag it through the mud.

*He runs to the camera, does a flip, and lands in
close-up.*

Is this your will?

Big orchestral crescendo.

Can you tell me why?

Dorothy sings the high note.

Why?

Jesus knocks her away, and resumes.

Why must I die?

He spins madly.

Tell me why a father would sacrifice a son?

He falls to the ground in despair.

Do you see a problem here?

He looks to the camera.

Or am I the only one?

He flips over and punches the ground.

I really, truly, really, truly, really don't want to die.

He spits sand out of his mouth and flips back up.

But if you insist, can you at least tell me why?

He rotates his arms in an impossible circle.

Why must I die?
Why?
Why?
Why must I die. Why must I—

> *Instrumental break. Rick places the soldiers around Jesus, arresting him. He places a George W. Bush 'Marine outfit' action figure amongst them. Finally, Judas—the Homer 'Pez' dispenser—is placed in the sand as the music comes to a dramatic stop. The song resumes quietly.*

I know you're here,
With me, within me.
Then why do I feel so alone?
I'm just a man.

> *Rick leans forward to the camera and tilts it up.*

I cannot fight them.
Because my will is not my own

> *The camera slowly lifts off the floor. Rick gets up with it and sings into it.*

I'll rise up to the challenge,
I'll take it like a man,
Who am I to question my Father's Holy Plan?

> *He walks downstage under the camera as it continues to ascend. He looks up, as if to God, and continues to sing.*

Your flesh and blood won't let you down.
Your son, I'll always be
A beaten, broken, bleeding man, if that's what
meant for me.

Musical climax.

If this be your will
Thy will be done.

> *Rick holds his last note. The song ends. He
> approaches a projector that sits on the floor at the
> front of the stage and pushes a button to turn it on.
> As he continues with the liturgy, the screen slowly
> rises behind him.*

Father, you are holy indeed, and all your
creation rightly gives you praise. All life, all
holiness comes from you through your Son,
Jesus Christ our Lord, by the working of the
Holy Spirit. From age to age, you gather a
people to yourself, so that from east to west
a perfect offering may be made to the glory
of your name. And so, Father, we bring you
these gifts. We ask you to make them holy
by the power of your Spirit, that they may
become the body and blood of your Son, our
Lord Jesus Christ, at whose command we
celebrate this Eucharist.

On the night he was betrayed, he took the
bread and gave you thanks and praise. He
broke the bread, gave it to his disciples, and
said:

> *Rick turns upstage as the lights shift. The screen is
> gone. A red light reveals a long table—an altar. On
> it are various Christian icons, crosses, candles, and
> a wig, beard and moustache. Rick begins to walk
> towards the altar. He recites the following liturgy in
> its original Latin form.*

Accipite et manducate ex hoc omnes

He removes his shirt and throws it on the floor.

Hoc est enim corpus meum.

He bends down at the altar and pulls out a white robe, which he slips over his head. A camera, hidden in the altar, is pointed at his face, which is projected onto the white surface of his back.

Simili modo postquam coenatum est,

He takes the chalice, removes the cloth that covers it, and wipes his brow.

Accipiens et hunc praeclarum calicem in sanctas ac venerabiles manus suas:

He takes a drink from the chalice.

Item tibi gratias agens, benedixit, deditque discipulis suis, dicens:

He replaces the chalice, opens a small jar, and applies spirit gum to his face.

Accipite et bibite ex co omnes: hic est enim calix sanguinis mei,

He affixes the beard.

Novi et aeterni testamenti: mysterium fidei, qui pro vobis et pro multis,

He affixes the moustache.

Effendetur in remissionem peccatorum.

He takes the Jesus wig and places it on his head.

Do this in memory of me.

He extends his arms, creating an even larger surface of white to project on. He chants:

Let us proclaim the mystery of faith: Christ has died, Christ is risen, Christ will come again.

Trial

The lights change suddenly. The projected image disappears. 'Gloria' from Mozart's Latin Mass plays loudly. Now dressed as Jesus, Rick turns and walks in silhouette towards the audience. The screen descends as Mozart plays. Jesus arrives downstage, his arms outstretched. The lights slowly rise on him. He silently looks at the audience. A clock ticks. Long pause.

Many men, claiming to speak for me, will come and say, 'I am he!' and, 'The time has come!' But don't follow them. Don't be afraid when you hear of wars and revolutions; such things must happen. Countries will fight each other; kingdoms will attack one another. There will be terrible earthquakes, famines, and plagues everywhere; there will be strange and terrifying things coming from the sky. But do not worry, because now the Son of Man's glory is revealed. Now God's glory is revealed through him. And if God's glory is revealed through him, then the glory of the Son of Man will be revealed in God himself, and he will do so at once. My children, I shall not be with you much longer. You will look for me. But you cannot go where I am going. And so I leave you with this new commandment: Love one another. As I have loved you, so you must love one another.

Long pause.

Any questions?

Pause. A cock crows.

Well, we still have some time…

Pause. The clock continues to tick.

You have heard it said, An eye for an eye, and a tooth for a tooth. But I say unto you, don't resist

evil: whoever strikes you on the right cheek…turn him the other as well.
Do unto others as you would have them do unto you.
Love your enemies…
Listen to your parents.
Don't worry, be happy.
Consistent dental hygiene is also very important.
Get along with your co-workers.
Don't sweat the small stuff.
Regular sex is good for the prostate.
And if thy right hand offend thee, cast it off.
Judge not lest ye be judged yourselves.
Always lift with your legs.
And Bob's your Uncle.

Pause.

Yep.

Pause.

He's back…

Jesus speaks in a 'movie-trailer' voice.

…and this time, he's playing it for laughs!
In a world of sin and despair, one man…no…
Sometimes, when the world gets you down…no…
The story of a man who came down from his cross, and changed the world forever.
Jesus II.

Pause.

So I'm standing there with Pilate, and he asks "Art thou a King then?" And I answer, "Thou sayest that I am a king. But to this end I was born and for this cause came I into the world, that I should bear witness unto the truth. Every one that is of the truth heareth my voice." And Pilate asks me, "What is truth?" And I say nothing. But what I'm thinking is that my mother will suffer as she watches me die a painful, terrible death. And my followers will die painful, terrible deaths, and their parents will suffer as they watch them die. There will be 300 years of suffering, but in that time, my followers will write beautiful, inspiring stories about me. And then, Constantine, a Roman general, a pagan, will claim to have seen a vision of a cross in the sky on his way to battle. My cross. Underneath the cross will be written "In this sign conquer". And conquer he will, in my name, turning my cross into a sword. He will call himself 'HOLY ROMAN EMPEROR.' Divine power on earth.

A cock crows.

And with this divine power, he will extend the reach of the Roman Empire, and unify the fractured Church of my followers through fear, through submission, and through liturgy. A liturgy created at the council of Nicea in the 4th Century. A liturgy of mysterious power and beauty that will define exactly who I am, and what my story is to be, once and for all, unchangeable. From that point on, I will no longer be Yeshua of Nazareth, son of Joseph, lover of Mary Magdalene, but Jesus-Christ, the Son of God, born of the Virgin Mary. Constantine will force this new story upon the Empire. Those who believe it will be saved, those who do not will be crushed. The new, unified Church will hunt down and eliminate all traces of its pagan past. There will be 200 years of forgery, fraud, book burning, character assassination, murder… And then we come to the Dark Ages. The Roman Empire will crumble, and Barbarians will take over Europe. The Church will survive, but will be split in two: the Church of the Popes in Rome, and the Church now called Orthodox, East of Rome. In my homeland, another religion will claim God unto itself for the purpose of Empire. It will be called Islam, and its followers will conquer the lands around Jerusalem, which means 'City of Peace'. My Church will feel threatened by this new religion, and will try to reclaim Jerusalem, and thus will begin the age of the Crusades, all fought in my name. After the Crusades will come the Wars of Religion, when my name will be used to further split the Church into those who still submit to Roman authority, and those who protest it, 'Protestants.' They will then sail across the seas to a New World, where my name will be used to wipe out entire civilizations, to wipe out their stories, songs and dances. The years will pass, and in my name more blood will be spilled, and bodies will continue to pile upon bodies... And yes, there will be lots of great deeds, and lots of great art and music, and lots of lovely buildings. Either way, Christ was used, Christ is being used right now, Christ will be used again. And that's fine. Really. Use me, abuse me. Use my image, my name, my corporate logo to justify your cause. There is no copyright issue. I'm public domain. Why fight it? Let's celebrate it. Simply log onto biggerthanj.com, and visit our 'Jesus Christ Superstore', where you'll find salvation on sale at low, discount prices. Brand Jesus.

Pause.

And I'm thinking all that as I stand there in front of Pilate. But I say nothing.

Pause. A cock crows.

I should go.

Pause.

I'm not very good at goodbyes, so...

He steps out of light. He steps back in again.

I'm back!
I should leave on a good note.

> *Pause. He sings a good note, and stops abruptly. He shakes his head. Pause.*

I should…uh…
Remember me.

> *He steps out of light.*

A-dieu.

> *A piano strikes—the first chord of Ravel's "Khaddisch." It plays on as Rick takes off the wig and robe. He kneels and holds them both in a pieta-like pose. He places them gently on to the floor, and continues with the liturgy.*

Father, we offer you in thanksgiving this holy and living sacrifice.

Look with favour on your Church's offering, and see the victim whose death has reconciled us to yourself. And grant that we, who are nourished by his body and blood, may become one body, one Spirit, in Christ.

Welcome into your kingdom our departed brothers and sisters, and all who have left this world in your friendship. We hope to enjoy for ever the vision of your glory, through Christ our Lord, from whom all good things come.

> *He reaches for the crown of thorns. As he lowers in on to his head, the camera begins to descend, projecting his image onscreen.*

Through him, with him, in him, in the unity of the Holy Spirit, all glory and honour is yours, almighty Father, for ever and ever. Amen.

And now, let us pray with confidence to the
Father in the words our Saviour gave us:

He turns to face the screen, his back to the camera.

Our Father, who art in heaven,

We hear the sound of a whip, very loud.

hallowed be thy name; thy kingdom come;
thy will be done on earth as it is in heaven.

Whip.

Give us this day our daily bread; and forgive
us our trespasses as we forgive those who
trespass against us;

Whip.

and lead us not to temptation, but deliver us
from evil.

*Two whips. He turns to face the camera, and
approaches it.*

For thine is the kingdom, the power and the
glory, now and forever, amen.

*He kicks the toys away from the sand pile. He tilts
the camera down until it points to the floor.*

Lord, Jesus Christ, you said to your apostles:
I leave you peace, my peace I give to you.
Look not on our sins, but on the faith of your
Church, and grant us the peace and unity of
your kingdom where you live for ever and
ever. Amen. The peace of the Lord be with
you always. And also with you.
Let us offer each other the sign of peace.

Crucifixion

A light appears on the floor forming a cross. Rick lies down on it in a crucifixion pose. He is projected onscreen.

Father, into your hands I commend my spirit.
It is finished.
Forgive me.

The camera slowly begins to zoom in on Rick's face, then his eyeball, then further. The image blurs. Pause. The camera begins to rise. The blurry image becomes clear again, revealing Rick's face. His eyes are closed. He is crucified. The camera rises into the lights and disappears. The image onscreen stops moving: it is the crucified Rick as seen from the heavens. Pause. Rick sits up but the image onscreen remains frozen. Rick kneels beside the pile of sand and slowly begins to play with it.

Lamb of God, you take away the sins of the world: have mercy on us.
Lamb of God, you take away the sins of the world: have mercy on us.
Lamb of God, you take away the sins of the world: grant us peace.

The image of the crucified Rick slowly fades. We now see Rick onscreen from above, drawing in the sand.

May this mingling of the body and blood of our Lord Jesus Christ bring eternal life to us who receive it.

This is the Lamb of God who takes away the sins of the world. Happy are those who are called to his supper.

Lord, I am not worthy to receive you, but only say the word and I shall be healed.

Resurrection

The sand drawing is finished. It is an image of the crucified Christ. Rick, in kneeling position, delivers the final words of the liturgy.

The Lord be with you.
May almighty God bless you, the Father,
and the Son, and the Holy Spirit.
The Mass is ended. Go in peace and love and
serve the Lord. Thanks be to God.

Lights fade to black, image fades to black.

The End.